Cold Steel Raw Truth About White Liberals & Race In USA

A BIG REASON WHY AFRICAN AMERICANS ARE NOT HELD ACCOUNTABLE AS A RACE IS BECAUSE OF LIBERAL PATRONIZING. THEY TEACH THEIR OWN KIDS RIGHT FROM WRONG AND HOLD THEM TO VERY HIGH STANDARDS AND SEND THEM TO THE BEST OF SCHOOLS.

BUT, AT THE SAME TIME ARE OUT FRONT TREATING AFRICAN AMERICANS LIKE THEY ARE AN INFERIOR RACE THAT CAN'T COPE. READILY PAMPERING AND MAKING EXCUSES BECAUSE OF SOMETHING HAPPENED 200 YEARS AGO, WHICH IS, MISPLACED BLAME IN MY VIEW.

I SAY NONE SENSE, POPPYCOCK, BEFORE THIS LIBERAL INDUCED WELFARE STATE AFRICAN AMERICANS GOT NO FAVORS AND EXPECTED NONE THEY EARNED WHAT THEY GOT SOMETIMES BEING THREE TIMES BETTER AT A TASK. DON'T INSULT MY INTELLIGENCE, AFRICAN AMERICANS CAN COPE AND OBEY THE LAW AS WELL AS ASIANS OR ANY RACE.

THERE IS NOTHING COMPLICATED

Cold Steel Raw Truth About White Liberals & Race In USA

ABOUT THIS MATTER, IT IS VERY SIMPLE, AFRICAN AMERICANS ARE NOT TEACHING THEIR YOUNG PROPER NORMS AND FAMILY TRADITIONS ON HOW TO BEHAVE AND ACT CIVILIZED. I REST MY CASE, LET THE JURY DECIDE.

SURE, THERE IS ALWAYS TWO SIDES TO EVERYTHING IN LIFE BUT WHERE YOU AIM YOUR FOCUS IS WHAT TRULY MATTERS. I KNOW THERE WILL ALWAYS BE SOME RACIALISM AS LONG AS WE HAVE DIFFERENT RACES.

THERE WILL ALWAYS BE A FEW OVERLY AGGRESSIVE POLICEMEN AS LONG AS WE HAVE POLICEMEN. IT IS THE FOCUS THAT SETS YOU FREE, WE AS AFRICAN AMERICANS HAVE NOT TOTALLY LEARNED HOW TO FORGIVE AND ACCEPT OURSELVES AND THOSE THAT LOOK LIKE US AS BEING AS GOOD AS ANY RACE UNCONDITIONALLY.

UNTIL WE DO THAT WE WILL BE FOREVER PLACING BLAME EVERYWHERE ELSE BUT WITH THE

MAN IN THE MIRROR. IT IS A FACT, TRUST AND RESPECT MUST BE EARNED OTHERWISE YOU REAP WHAT YOU SOW. FOLKS, I'M A WRITER, THAT IS ALL, I HAVE NO POWER TO CHANGE ANYTHING, YOU BELIEVE AS YOU CHOOSE. I HAVE HAD MY SAY. GOD BLESS.

INJECTION #2: 22 DECEMBER 2014, 1406 HOURS

CAN THE USA SURVIVE IRRESPONSIBLE LEADERS THAT DOESN'T SUPPORT THE RULE OF LAW AND THOSE THAT ENFORCE THE LAW. THOSE THAT EXCUSE LAW BREAKERS ARE WEAK AND LACK THE DISCIPLINE TO BE GOOD LEADERS IN MY VIEW. THAT DON'T MEAN WE ARE NOT A FORGIVING PEOPLE.

THE USA CAN'T SAVE ITSELF; ONLY REPEALING THE EVIL 1938 SOCIALIST MINIMUM WAGE LAW WILL LET THE USA ECONOMY KICK ASS AND SAVE OUR GREAT NATION. MAN CAN'T DO

Cold Steel Raw Truth About White Liberals & Race In USA

IT.

THE REAL PROBLEM IS WE THE PEOPLE HAVE LOST THIS GREAT COUNTRY BECAUSE OF SHALLOW MINDED LIBERALS AND LIBERALISM. NOW, THE QUESTION IS HOW DO WE THE PEOPLE TAKE IT BACK, WE CAN'T, BUT THE ECONOMY CAN. AND THE ECONOMY CAN ONLY DO IT BY BECOMING FREE OF THE SHACKLES OF THE CRUEL EVIL 1938 SOCIALIST MINIMUM WAGE LAW.

SURE, ON THE SURFACE A MINIMUM WAGE LAW SEEMS LIKE A GOOD THING BUT IT IS A DAGGER IN THE HEART OF A FREE MARKET PLACE ECONOMY AND RENDERS IT HELPLESS TO FIGHT OFF INFLATION. ALSO, IT ROTS AWAY THE INNER FABRIC OF A NATION UNTIL IT IS MORALLY BANKRUPT.

EXCEPT, OUR LEARNED ECONOMIST AND EGG HEADS DON'T CALL THE

Cold Steel Raw Truth About White Liberals & Race In USA

DESTRUCTIVE FLAW IN OUR ECONOMY INFLATION, THEY CALL IT GROWTH WHICH IS THE BIGGEST LIE THAT HAS EVER BEEN TOLD. I'M ONE THAT IS NOT FOOLED FOR A SECOND, "YOU CAN'T FOOL ALL OF THE PEOPLE ALL OF THE TIME."

INJECTION #1: 14 DECEMBER 2014, 1430 HOURS

Churchill said it best, I'm paraphrasing, "Trying to tax your way out of debt is like standing in a bucket and trying to lift it by the handle."

LIFE IS A BLESSING, NO ONE TRULY KNOWS WHAT TOMORROW MAY BRING, WE ALL DANCE TO THE TUNE OF A DISTANCE DRUMMER

By all reasons I shouldn't be a writer but for some unknown force here I am putting pen to paper. My beloved homeland is in far more trouble than meet the eye of most Americans. We are over

Cold Steel Raw Truth About White Liberals & Race In USA

$18,000,000,000,000,000,000 in debt and it is still growing by leaps and bounds.

We are on a sure course to doom; yet we act like sleep walkers by growing our entitlement welfare state even bigger. Folks, I'm going to do something I don't like to do because I think it is self-serving, share secrets and talk about me and my inner self and beliefs.

Here goes, I may look normal, but I am not and never will be. As long as I can remember I have viewed myself as a mentally handicapped cripple. I hate the limelight, and doing anything out front in public. Sure, a few times I have been compelled to be out front but I will always avoid it at all cost.

I will never take a leadership role out front in public because I suffer from several neurotic symptoms. The first neurotic symptom I experienced was

Cold Steel Raw Truth About White Liberals & Race In USA

when I was around 5 or 6 years old, it started as a result of being whipped for wetting the bed.

I never took it personal or held it against my dad; he believed I was too lazy to get up which was not that uncommon many, many years ago. Anyway, it saddled me with a helpless neurotic pitiful look type symptom that would take over my brain like an epilepsy seizure right before getting those whippings.

Once the symptom started the pitiful look was not limited to just before getting a whipping the symptom could take over my brain in other situations especially if I was tired or before a large crowd of strangers. Over the years I have stayed out of situations that may trip a take over.

I'm telling it now, but most people that have known me all of my 72 years here on earth never knew this about

Cold Steel Raw Truth About White Liberals & Race In USA

me. The mind is a very power thing and especially with a young child, a bad trauma imprint can last a lifetime.

Sure, now I have the courage to face and talk about this condition and it doesn't affect me hardly ever anymore. But, I know it is lurking deep in my brain and can still take it over and render me helpless in certain situations.

No one has to tell me how it feels to be humiliated, ridiculed, laughed at, rejected, and on and on, at some time in my life I have experienced it all. But, above it all I believe the saying is true: That what don't kill you will make you stronger. Plus, I learned at a young age those that can genuine love and forgive cannot be mentally destroyed.

Some has tried to do just that to me for whatever reason is beyond me but I am still standing. You name it, hidden cameras, listening devices, GPS tracking, and on and on, yet I am still standing, even when no stone is left unturned. However, who knows what tomorrow may bring, all I know to do is keep pounding my stress call for the survival of my homeland.

I feel it is my destiny to keep sounding the distress call to repeal the cruel evil 1938 socialist minimum wage law entirely. I know 98 percent of the nation's population disagrees with me on this. But, that doesn't prove me wrong; practically all the nation's entire infrastructure like city water and sewage systems, bridges etc. was built before the 1938 minimum wage law.

Nothing else can save the USA from a total economic collapse in my view. And if that happened the government wouldn't have the money to pay these millions upon millions of people depending solely on the government. And if anybody thinks that can't happen he is a fool.

Cold Steel Raw Truth About White Liberals & Race In USA

Getting rid of the 1938 socialist minimum wage law will in a controlled way relieve the government of carrying the awesome debt burden of being a social and family provider. With no minimum wage law the people will be able to depend on themselves for survival, not a government already broke and 18 trillion in debt.

I have fought to survive all of my life and I'm telling you the 1938 minimum wage law must be repealed entirely. And to those that don't want to give up any power, you will not have any power anyway if this entitlement welfare state totally collapses. It's going to collapse, there is no doubt about that, exactly when no one knows, but, it may be much sooner than later.

It's just impossible for any nation to survive long term as a super social and family provider, period. It breaks all of the laws of economics. Churchill said it best, I'm paraphrasing, "Trying to tax your way out of debt is like standing in a bucket and trying to lift it by the handle."

Now, I will say something basically the same in my way: Government as a super social and family provider is like a country eating its young, therefore feeding on itself. Also, it is like eating your seed corn and drinking your priming water, which is dumb and stupid.

We have around 81 years of our sinister liberal democrat entitlement welfare state and its cost to the government is increasing at warp speed. This cost and debt burden to any government simply can't be sustained. Besides, this liberal shallow brained power grabbing idea of taking on such a cost in the first place for more than on a temporary basis was insane.

Cold Steel Raw Truth About White Liberals & Race In USA

Its not only the cost of such a hair brained idea, its effect has left millions upon millions of people dependent minded with no sense of accountability. It has ripped apart this great nation's culture and whole inner fabric to no end.

It has all but destroyed our once strong nuclear and extended family system that has secured the survival of human kind since the dawn of history. Now, when this welfare state government does go belly up all of the millions upon millions of dependents with no sense of responsibility or accountability have little to no chance of survival.

Its too late now, only repealing the evil 1938 socialist minimum wage law entirely can give this great nation a fighting chance of surviving, period. But, only a miracle can make that happen, if I alone seem to have the wisdom to see the light, so be it. Amen.

SIRMANS LOG: 13 DECEMBER 2014, 1541 HOURS

SECOND INJECTION: 10 DECEMBER 2014, 0755 HOURS:
I BELIEVE AIRING DIRTY LINEN IN PUBLIC DISPLAYS WEAKNESS, SHALLOW MINDNESS, AND A WEAK SURVIVAL INSTINCT, THERE IS NO VIRTUE IN THAT, CAN THE USA SURVIVE?

Every country is involved in this dark secret cloak and dagger stuff. The reason we have a republic form of government is because depending on the general public is the same as mob rule that is why the founding fathers wanted us to depend on those we elect to make responsible decisions.

The first rule in anything secret should be to tell only those that have a need to know. There is no need for the general public to know how the intelligence agency sausage is made, that is what we elect our Supposedly

Cold Steel Raw Truth About White Liberals & Race In USA

responsible leaders for.

In my view only a nation in an almost complete moral and economic decline would tell something so self-destructive. God, I ask in your name, save America from itself. I swear!!!

I take no side in this matter, my point is this sort of dirty linen should be fought out and dealt with out of the public limelight. Many other country does the same thing and far worse. We are not fooling anyone, other countries knows what we are about.

They know what we are doing by exposing this, it shows weakness and self-serving. A great power and country shouldn't have a need to be loved, which is a weakness. And exposing something like this on the public stage equals a need to be loved like we are so good and holy. Now, being respected is a far different matter.

FIRST INJECTION: 04 DECEMBER 2014, 0845 HOURS
WE AFRICAN AMERICANS INSTEAD OF

Cold Steel Raw Truth About White Liberals & Race In USA

ACCEPTING OURSELVES AS A RACE UNCONDITIONALLY, WE STILL SUBCONSCIOUSLY WANT THE WHITE SLAVE MASTER IDENTIFY.

WE STILL HAVE NOT BROKEN THE CHAIN THAT WILL FREE US TO BE INDEPENDENT MINDED THINKERS; A HERD MENTALITY STILL CONTROLS US.

OBEDIENCE OF THE LAW MUST BE THE FIRST PRIORITY; FAILURE TO DO SO LEAVES NO EXCUSE FOR WHATEVER MAY HAPPEN
we all care about our loved ones. But, the only thing that keeps us from behaving like wild animals in the jungle is the law. The law must be above all else and the top priority for the USA to remain a civilized nation.

The law must be respected and obeyed, period. We now have the law flaunted and disrespected in high places, and after years of our liberal entitlement welfare state many have succumbed to raw subjective emotionalism. Whatever happened to the words "No one is above the law,"

Cold Steel Raw Truth About White Liberals & Race In USA

are they still valid?

You may want to be weak and stupid and live by the rules of the jungle with little or no respect for the law then have at it, just don't include me. I believe in "First things first," period. The law is what protects us all, especially the poor and disadvantage.

Part of what's wrong with this entitlement welfare state now is we have turned into a P.... society with less and less accountability. And it's going to be our downfall, you mark my word. Anyone that succumbs to the weakness of subjective emotionalism is a fool and loser, and is either ignorant or not dealing with a full deck in my view.

If one doesn't love and support unconditional one's own race he is without a true identity and can't really be trusted. It's a fact we African Americans are without a true identity and is searching for love in all of the wrong places. I've heard the chant, black and proud and all of that, but in my view it is just words and lack substance.

We need to believe we as African Americans are as good as any race and need to take pride in behaving and obeying the law as well as any race. If you want to be treated with respect, then act like one deserving respect. I believe we as a race can behave and obey the law as well as any race, and we as a race did too before our liberal entitlement welfare state came about. **SIRMANS LOG: 04 DECEMBER 2014, 1658 HOURS**

WE AFRICAN AMERICANS HAS A PRIMITIVE HERD MENTALITY WITH VERY LITTLE FREE INDEPENDENT ACCOUNTABILITY THINKING AMONG US

Most African Americans have a bond to the democrat party like a child to its mother. And no amount of reasoning or logic can break that bond unless the child becomes a free independent minded thinker. Nature's law of "taking the course of least resistance" dictates

Cold Steel Raw Truth About White Liberals & Race In USA

that almost no one is going to become a free independent accountability thinker unless forced to.

The herd won't allow free independent accountability thinking within the herd itself and even when an individual does it anyway he is branded a traitor or nut case. Hell, I love my country the only home I know and I feel if you are wrong you deserve to be called out even if you are a sister, brother, or mother.

I don't believe in pampering anyone, you are responsible for your own actions. To err is human, and forgiveness is the foundation of the Christian religion in my view. I'm one that believes that civilization would never have gotten out of the Dark Age without the Christian religion and its power of forgiveness.

My God, I watch the local news almost everyday and its smash and grab, armed robbery, breaking and interring, muggings, and crime galore. And guess who is doing almost all of this crime? You fill in the blank. Yet, all I hear from white liberals and black liberals is patronizing and misplaced guilt and no accountability what so ever, it's insane.

Before the "New deal" a trip behind the shed or woodpile would always keep the would be future criminals on the straight and narrow good citizen course and out of prison. Since that's not done very much any more the best thing that would do the most good for young future black criminals would be medical supervised flogging.

Four or five hard lick on the ass would do far more good than 5-10 in the pen and it wouldn't cost the taxpayers. That would put a stop to this paying to produce a more harden and cunning criminal. But, that will never happen, oh, no, we are too civilized for that, yet, the cancer of crime is splitting this great country into racial camps, duh.

Only one thing can save the great USA now: repeal the cruel evil 1938 socialist minimum wage law, then there will be no government forced wage control. That would get rid of any forced wage control entirely. That is the only way this great nation can be saved from itself, period. Repeal it now tomorrow may be too late.

SIRMANS LOG: 30 NOVEMBER 2014, 2123 HOURS

INJECTION: 02 DECEMBER 2014, 1232 HOURS
A huge disadvantage with African Americans having a herd mentality is it has allows a very few poverty pimps to exploit and keep alive this still-a-victim big, big, big, lie. And as long as we have our liberal induced welfare state I see very little chance of African Americans ever being forced to take

responsibility and stand on their own to gain a do-and-think-for-yourself mentality.

Sure, I may be hated for my views now, but there will come a day when I will be loved for my great wisdom and foresight, glory be to God.

Just look at our African American situation, in some neighborhoods there is not a husband to be found for miles. And even if you can find a man living in some of the homes all he is there for is companionship and stud service at her whim. Uncle Sam is the real sugar daddy, a poor man can't compete. Come on y'all give me a break now, instead of all of this rioting we as a race ought to be cleaning up our own house.

We ought to be instilling in our young discipline and self-respect and respect for other people and their property, too. Shame on us for not knowing how

Cold Steel Raw Truth About White Liberals & Race In USA

to behave and obey the law like other races does. Other races have eyes; they see who is committing all of these crimes. Reality is reality, don't insult my intelligence.

Sure, we as race are guilty of keeping a child's mentality including a fierce sibling rivalry against those who look like us. That is why African Americans can't advance as a race; we won't readily support each other in business or otherwise unless there is no other good choice. And even our elites will try to get as far away from an all black neighborhood as they can afford.

All other races create different pecking order level surrounding zones in their own race's community, lets face facts, and it takes an independent minded adult to escape childhood sibling rivalry. And the first thing it takes to do that is the ability to forgive all people. Otherwise, un-forgiveness locks one in to that situation, and then

Cold Steel Raw Truth About White Liberals & Race In USA

if one is still hating and un-forgiving seventy years later they will still have that fierce dependent minded sibling rivalry from childhood.

To escape here is a simple formula to repeat to yourself over and over until you mean it: "I can wish all people goodwill (through God who strengthens me), optional if you are a Christian." That will free one to become an independent thinker.

I never intended to get sidetracked off into all of this theory stuff, it seems as if my pen took on a life of its own, sorry. Sure, we as a race have some guilt in my view, but again the real arch villain behind the scene is the heavy hand of our liberal induced welfare state beast pulling the strings.

However, before the new deal African Americans had almost thrown off their dependency minded slave mentality, but the welfare state nipped all of that in the bud. Before the new deal blacks supported each other, and we had poor, middle class, and upper class zones in the same community. Plus, we had far more black owned businesses than today. Every town had a booming chitin's circuit and great entertainment.

We were about to become of age. But, the New deal kicked the poor black man out of the house. After that no one instilled discipline, proper norms, and traditions in our young and we lost our way. After all of that our dependency minded slave mentality returned with a vengeance and the democrat party and the welfare state is now our new slave masters.

SIRMANS LOG: 02 DECEMBER 2014, 1232 HOURS

FERGUSON IS A WAKE-UP CALL ON WHAT CULTURE ROT AND MORAL DECAY HAS DONE TO THE USA DUE

Cold Steel Raw Truth About White Liberals & Race In USA

TO OUR LIBERAL INDUCED WELFARE STATE

NEW INJECTION #2, 25 NOVEMBER 2014, 1907 HOURS

What we African Americans need to realize is each of us is an ambassador for our race. Many years ago we blacks knew that, but that seems to be lost now a days. A good or bad stereotype image affects all of us in some way, you can't escape it.

Call it what you may but there is no denying the fact that African Americans are committing far more crimes than any race on earth proportional-wise. The main reason for that is lack of parents instilling self-restraint and self-accountability in their young. A lack of self-restraint and self-accountability breeds disrespect for authority and the rights of others.

That is what's driving this out of

Cold Steel Raw Truth About White Liberals & Race In USA

control cancer in the African American community call crime. But, the actual real villain driving everything from behind the curtain is our liberal induced welfare state beast, with the ability to throw a rock and hide its hand. I stand by my prediction that the USA economy will collapse in 2015 unless our cruel evil 1938 socialist minimum wage law is repealed.

I see all of the economically ignorant do-gooders believing that raising the minimum wage will help people, but in reality it will only speed up our pace to an economy collapsing doom. Getting rid of any wage or price control entirely is our only way out, because that will restore power back to the people then the people will need very little money and live off the land if need to.

However, there has never been a case of government changing course knowing it is headed to doom; it is not in its DNA. The power that be is going to feed this tax hungry gobbling welfare state beast to the last crumb.

They will never stop feeding the beast and I will never stop drum beating to repeal our evil 1938 socialist minimum wage law to save the only home and way of life I know. Glory be to God.

SIRMANS LOG: 25 NOVEMBER 2014, 1907 HOURS

NEW INJECTION: 24 NOVEMBER 2014, 0853 HOURS

Never in the history of mankind has the poor ever been liberal and moral corrupted until the "New deal" programs created a baby welfare state around 81 years ago. Now we have more poor killing babies in the womb and neutralizing their seed in other ways than any demographic group. No hardship or struggle breed's liberalism and a weak survival instinct.

Anyone with a strong survival instinct

Cold Steel Raw Truth About White Liberals & Race In USA

(like me) will instinctly know the unborn must be protected for the long-term survival of the species. The fact is the USA simply cannot and will not survive unless the cruel evil 1938 socialist minimum wage law is repealed. Any and all types of wage or price controls must be removed entirely.

That will set the all-powerful free market place free to save the USA and western civilization, too. Look at the immigration problem in the USA and around the world, it's going to engulf us, there is no human solution.

However, if the USA free market were set free by repealing the evil 1938 socialist minimum wage law, then a genuine true free market place armed with nature's supreme law of natural selection would solve the problem and save the USA and western civilization, too.

SIRMANS LOG: 24 NOVEMBER

2014, 0853 HOURS

PS: I believe they are really fixing to financially knife and gut our beloved military like never before.

WE AFRICAN AMERICANS ARE NOW TREATED LIKE A BUCK TOOTH REDHEADED STEP CHILD BY THE DEMS

Political speaking African Americans are now the redheaded step child of the Democrat party. This child has a dependency slave mentality and is totally loyal to his/her caretaker. Yet, this child's dependency and loyalty is taken for granted. And now a new adoptee is being favored and groomed ahead of this child, sad, sad.

This child loves and wants to be just like his caretaker in every way. This dependent child sees the complexion of his caretaker and feels that represents the ideal way one need to be.

Cold Steel Raw Truth About White Liberals & Race In USA

However, when the child looks in the mirror he doesn't look like his caretaker physically but mentally wants to be as much like his caretaker as possible. Plus, this dependent child sees others that look like him as competitors, or even the enemy in winning the most favorite one's role by his caretaker. That is why African Americans won't readily support each other in businesses or otherwise if there is a choice. And the beat continues on, as long as this child retains his slave dependency mentality he will not escape his predicament, ever.

The only way out and for this child to acquire free objective independent thinking is to shed his dependent slave mentality. That is a lot easier said than done. It is much easier to follow the herd than to veer off into the unknown and entirely fend for yourself. Also, to take that giant step it is almost impossible when there is a welfare state promising to take care of all in need from cradle to grave.

To take the course of least resistance is embedded in us all. The only thing that is going to get African Americans to be free thinker and independent minded is for the crutch to be kicked from under us. To hell with the victimized mentality, its time African Americans take responsibility individually and as a race and feel responsible for their own survival.

Its time we pull up our pants and face down bad behavior, we know right from wrong, enough of this kindergarten blame, blame, blame game. This cancer crime is out of control in our race and we act like its someone else's problem. There was a time when we blacks had self-respect and behaved as well as any race of people. Why should the Dems treat us with respect, they will continually throwing us a bone every now and then and keep treating us like a buck tooth redheaded stepchild.

If not for this sinister welfare state African Americans would have long ago shed our dependency slave mentality and still have mostly two parent families.

SIRMANS LOG: 22 NOVEMBER 2014, 1406 HOURS

MOB RULE, MOB RULE, MOB RULE!!!

Mob rule the very thing the founding fathers feared the most has now come to past. Political polling is just a fancy name for mob rule. We now have out of control do-good emotionalism, while economic ignorance abounds. The law is now treated like an ass.

Folks, we have now arrived. Lord I ask in your name, have mercy on our ignorant souls. And the really sad part is the USA is still the economic engine of the world global economy. And, if the USA economy collapses the world global economy will bite the dust, too. That is all she wrote.

Folks, nothing I say is written in stone, but mark my words the USA economy will collapse in the year of our Lord 2015. It's too late, nothing can stop it, the stars are aligned and the bust cycle must complete its rotation to make room for the next boom cycle.

Nothing, not even repealing the cruel evil 1938 socialist minimum wage law entirely can stop the collapse. However, repealing the evil 1938 socialist minimum wage law entirely is the only thing that will allow the USA and western civilization to live through this coming collapsing doom.

Otherwise, modern industrial civilization regresses back to the Stone Age. Nature's die has been cast. Dismiss my great supernatural wisdom

Cold Steel Raw Truth About White Liberals & Race In USA

if you may, we'll soon see.
SIRMANS LOG: 21 NOVEMBER 2014, 1032 HOURS

SOME PLAIN HONEST POLITICAL TALK BY GREAT WRITER FREDDIE L SIRMANS SR.
Folks, I just felt like doing some plain honest political talk on the status and future the USA. I guess everyone knows that talk radio is dominated by so called conservatives. And let me say up front that at heart I consider myself a conservative, but above all I am a realist.

Sure, I must admit that I am somewhat bias in favor of the conservative view, but to me political extremism is dangerous and counterproductive from the right the same as from the left. I think there is a world of difference between the conservatives of today and the conservatives of the founding father's day.

I think the conservatives in their day had far more wisdom than exist today.

Cold Steel Raw Truth About White Liberals & Race In USA

In fact in their day almost everyone was conservative. Back then just day to day living demanded one be a conservative if one wanted to survive. Nature and the elements were harsh and unforgiving which left little opportunity for liberalism to breed.

An easy life and something for nothing is what is necessary for liberalism to breed. Before our "New deal" liberal created welfare state conservatives were men of great wisdom and depth with super strong survive instincts, not these shallow minded liberal like P . . . . . that abounds today.

Many of the founding fathers were born in Europe and had seen first hand what an all-powerful government would do. Now, let's fast-forward to today's conservatives. Most of the conservatives of today are just as shallow minded as the liberals, and with weak survival instincts, too.

I will keep it simple; there is no way to instill the necessary proper character in human beings without at least a minimum amount of hardship and struggle, period. Human being has evolved over millions of years and survived aided with an instinct to survive. So, as a rule the harder the struggle and hardship the stronger the instinct to survive. The least amount of hardship and struggle the weaker ones survival instinct will be.

No one acquires the almost supernatural survival instinct I have without some type of great hardship and struggle, mine has been an internal mental battle almost all of my life against self-shame, self-guilt, and things of the sort. However, there is always an exception to everything in life.

The same goes for hardship and struggle, it will make most human beings a better person or even a saint, but a few will become the bitterest one can become. Our liberal induced welfare state has almost completely destroyed our once strong culture and nuclear family system. No one has to tell me this welfare state is over; by instinct I just know it.

I also just know that the social and family provider role must be returned to the people if this great nation is to survive. I also know that our welfare state beast and the powers that be will never voluntarily surrender the social and family provider role back to the people.

That is the reason for my all out assault on the cruel evil 1938 socialist minimum wage law, its repeal is the only vehicle that can wrest the social and family provider role from the government back to the people, and save this great nation from total ruins. I didn't expect the shallow minded liberals to have the depth or wisdom to understand my writing, but I have found that today's conservatives fare little better.

SIRMANS LOG: 18 NOVEMBER 2014, 0038 HOURS

MEMO #2: OBAMACARE WILL COLLAPSE USA ECONOMY IN 2015

You can't turn back the test of time, the horse has left the barn, the ship has sailed, the train has left the station, you can't put the tooth paste back in the tube, the fat lady has sung, the s... has hit the fan; the cat is out of the bag, the chickens has flew the coop, a day late and a dollar short, and no sense in crying over spilt milk. Those are some metaphors concerning Obamacare.

I predict Obamacare is the straw that is going to break the camels back in 2015, meaning the USA economy. It is going to destroy the best medical system to ever exist. The die has been cast and there is no undoing the damage.

The profit from the USA government survival host (USA businesses) simply can't support its parasite financial load any longer, the load is simply just too great, the economy will collapse in 2015. But, there is a glimmer of hope to keep from losing it all.

The cruel evil 1938 socialist minimum wage law must be repealed to prevent a total collapse all the way back to the Stone Age. And I pray to God that I am

totally wrong on this.
UPDATE:
Ever since the "New deal" politicians to buy votes has added layer upon layer of taxes and fees to the cost of doing business. Its over folks, this welfare state beast is not going to tolerate going on a diet. There could be mass civil unrest in 2015 unless the cruel evil 1938 socialist minimum wage law is repealed.

Repealing that evil 1938 socialist minimum wage law will relieve the awesome heavy financial burden load of government being a social and family provider. With no minimum wage law the people will be able to afford providing for themselves.

The economy will then be free with no limit to growth, but on the other hand it may be possible to buy a week worth of grocery for $5.00. Freedom baby, that's what I'm talking about, being able to eat and survive baby.

SIRMANS LOG: 11 NOVEMBER 2014, 1703 HOURS

Cold Steel Raw Truth About White Liberals & Race In USA

AHOY, AHOY, SHIP AHOY AND FAREWELL TO OUR WELFARE STATE!

Folks, I'm a writer and I know much of my writing seem far-fetched, so, accept it as food for thought. OK, let all of the pundits have their say, but you know what they say about opinions, they are like x we all have one. I give my congratulation to the republicans for their great landslide win. Now, you have become like a co-captain to this vastly overloaded slowly sinking welfare state ship.

You have a very, very serious dilemma; this ship is sinking and has very important and needed cargo on board. Much of the cargo is needed for maintenance to keep the ship afloat. To just start cutting and slashing and throwing things overboard may be counterproductive, but the overloaded sinking of the ship must be stopped, and now.

The republicans don't know what to do, nether does the pundits. Enough on the sinking ship analogy; lets get down to some brass tacks. With my supernatural wisdom I believe nothing can stop the USA economy from collapsing, except repealing the evil 1938 socialist minimum wage law, period.

I believe the republican are going to start cutting social programs and that would be the worst course to take at this stage. It will make the economy worse and cause even more frustration. In fact it may be a good thing the republicans doesn't control the presidency at this time. That is because overall the establishment republicans thinking are just as faulty as the liberals and Dems.

Just like the dems and almost all of the USA population think our welfare state can be saved, wrong, it's far too late for that. The republicans think they can fine-tune our welfare state beast by doing a little cutting here and there and stimulating the economy to get jobs popping, wrong. This monster welfare state beast is going to chew the republicans up and spit them out.

Cold Steel Raw Truth About White Liberals & Race In USA

You just watch, in the next two years I just don't believe anything is going to improve. Of course, I hope I'm wrong on this. I'm sure the only thing that is going to prevent the USA economy from a total collapse in 2015 is to repeal the 1938 minimum wage law. You see humans are motivated and controlled by self-interest. Man can't control nature. Nature's supreme law of natural selection is what actually controls an economy.

Sure, mans actions can greatly influence the economy, but sooner or later every economy is going to complete a boom and bust cycle whether man likes it or not. Man can't stop a long over due bust cycle that is the result of our minimum wage law. But, if the USA untie and free the economy of this insane wage law it will allow us to live through the cycle without a total collapse back to the Stone Age.

The root problem with the USA economy is the liberals has crippled and tied it up by enacting this cruel evil 1938 socialist minimum wage law. That weakens the USA economy where it has no power to fight off inflation or discipline itself. Nothing is going to save the USA economy until it is set free. Otherwise nothing can stop our economy from collapse in 2015.

So, nothing the republicans can do that will truly make much difference unless they free and unbind the USA economy by repealing the 1938 minimum wage law. The establishment republicans like the Dems will try to keep our welfare state beast fed but will fail. And my guess is the liberals and Dems will come roaring back in 2016 with a vengeance and the republicans will be booted out.

One way or another welfare states as super family providers is over and the sooner the USA and western civilization faces that fact the better off we all will be. The first liberal mistake was making the government take on the financial burdens of becoming a permanent social and family provider, because once dependency takes root it is virtually impossible to uproot it.

So, if man can't undo this mistake then free the economy to do the job. Repealing the 1938 socialist minimum wage law will kill two birds with one stone. It will allow the economy to cut off the money supply to our destructive false daddy provider role, and second free the USA economy to kick ass and do what it takes to save our great nation.

A true untied free market place economy with unhindered competition has never in history failed to produce an over abundance of everything a nation need (Jobs).
SIRMANS LOG: 05 NOVEMBER 2014, 1839 HOURS

POLITICAL POLLING DEFEATS THE PURPOSE OF HAVING A REPUBLIC FORM OF GOVERNMENT
I know it's not going to happen, but political polling should be banned at least three months before every major political election.

The reason is it defeats the purpose of having a republic form of government in the first place. The founding fathers to a man all agreed that a republic form of government was best because pure democracy was nothing more than mob rule.

It is true today as it was well over 200 years ago that the general public as a rule is uninformed, emotional, and has a herd instinct. But, one thing the founding fathers didn't know and had no conception of was scientific polling. Instead of the general public voting directly on major decisions governing the country a republic would choose leaders to make those decisions.

The chosen leaders would be elected on what they individually believed and campaigned on, period. That way important decisions governing the country would be insulated from unsound emotional mob rule. That worked just fine until scientific polling came along.

Political polling in my view is nothing more than a fancy name for mob rule. And right now out right mob rule is in total control political-wise. This has

Cold Steel Raw Truth About White Liberals & Race In USA

allowed the shallow minded irresponsible liberals to exploit the negative emotional weaknesses in our human makeup, which has all but destroyed this great nation.

They have given away the store and promised everyone pie in the sky from cradle to grave. It is the biggest lie that has ever been told. Government must never, and I mean never take on more than a temporary family provider role if any nation is to survive.

It may take as much as eighty years or more, but the destruction die will have been cast. The financial burdens of the family provide role just becomes too heavy for any government to carry. Plus, no nation can survive very long without a strong nuclear and extended family system, which government as a family provider will totally destroy.

Nature's supreme law of natural selection is based on a survival need. Anything in nature without a survival need starts ceasing to exist. Government as family provider takes away the survival need for the private sector nuclear and extended family system until it ceases to exist.

There never has and never will be a society that last over 80-100 years without a strong nuclear and extended family system. It's just not possible because the most critical thing in having a stable long lasting society is instilling proper norms and traditions in the young. And that can't be done without a strong male disciplinarian as head of household, case close. Of course there is always an exception to everything in life.

Government playing daddy just doesn't cut the mustard. The USA economy will collapse in 2015 unless the evil 1938 socialist minimum wage law is repealed. If you think I'm crazy and don't know what I'm talking about, your wait won't be very long, we'll see before 2015 is over. And if I'm wrong I'll gladly eat crow.

SIRMANS LOG: 02 NOVEMBER 2014, 1209 HOURS

Cold Steel Raw Truth About White Liberals & Race In USA

CAT CALLS AND WOLF WHISTLING GONE TO THE EXTREME!

I saw the video on TV of the woman that walked three blocks in the Big Apple. And I must admit that I was a little taken aback by the amount of catcalls and wolf whistling that took place. Sure, catcalls and wolf whistling has always been around especially with men in Europe. But, never like what seem to be taking place in the USA today.

The reason I decided to weigh in on this is because it is a reflection of the moral decay and culture rot that is destroying this great nation. It is the result of our liberal induced welfare state. Government seizing the burden of the social and family provider role for itself and enacting the 1938 minimum wage law, that has ripped the moral fabric of the USA to threads. And the really sad part is very few seem to have the survival instinct or wisdom to give a damn.

There is more to this extreme amount of cat calling and wolf whistling than meet the eye in my view. Before our welfare state this type of behavior was mostly limited to a very very few aggressive males or groups of males. Construction crews have long been known for this type behavior but never over doing it.

Groups of males like to do this sort of thing I believe to make some kind of kinky macho statement, and to impress other males if anything. But, I'm going to give you the real skinny on what I believe has happen to the minds of a lot of men today. Sure, due to our welfare state the USA culture and morals are shot all to hell, but porn is slowly nailing the lid shut on our coffin.

I believe due to porn a lot of men just don't have respect for women like in the days of old. And I think this extreme amount of cat calling and wolf whistling has an element of contempt and disrespect if more so than admiration.

SIRMANS LOG: 30 OCTOBER 2014, 1953 HOURS

Cold Steel Raw Truth About White Liberals & Race In USA

Government carrying the load burden of social and family provider must end, now. This republic must end this ignorant shallow minded liberal lifetime load burden placed on our government with good intentions. "The road to hell is paved with good intentions."

Sure, after the nuclear and extended family, churches, and social organizations, and as a last resort on a temporary basis government aid is a must. But, to take on permanently a burden that has been with the private sector for over 6,000 years to me is just plain economic ignorance.

Every penny the government survives on comes from the private sector and every dependent the government adds on is one less private sector taxpayer, duh. Doing that means it is only a matter of time before the well dries up. That is where the USA and western civilization stands today.

Everyone standing around waiting on big government to provide for them from cradle to grave is a very, very dangerous thing in my view. The bigger government grows the smaller its provider private sector host dwindles until the whole thing collapses. That is what's fixing to happen to this P . . . . of an economy the USA have today.

The only thing that can and will save the USA economy is to repeal the evil cruel 1938 socialist minimum wage law. Any wage or price control is socialist and it ties up and cripples a free market place where it can't purge out inflation, waste, moral decay, and inefficiency.

All that is necessary to save the USA is to repeal the minimum wage law and set the free market free. Then just be still, the free market will take it from there. There is nothing on earth economically wise more powerful than a true unrestricted free market place economy with unlimited competition.

With no plus or minus wage or price controls the free market place will save the USA and western civilization. However, it won't be pretty because a lot of waste, moral decay and inefficiency must be purged in the process. That is the choice the USA faces; otherwise, to stay on course and do nothing means a sure collapse and doom.

Who knows after that, it may mean all the way back to the Stone Age? A true unrestricted free market place economy with unlimited competition has never in the history of mankind failed to produce far more jobs and everything than a nation need.
SIRMANS LOG: 16 OCTOBER 2014, 1149 HOURS.

WHY I THINK THE USA HAS A P . . . . OF AN ECONOMY?
The downfall and coming doom of the USA can all be traced to the economy. Sure, we are a nation ruled by law instead of men, but contrary to what almost everyone thinks the economy is the ultimate ruler in a free country.

Authoritarian countries can rule with an iron fist and demand people toe the party line or else. But, in free nations people have the freedom to disagree, disobey, and to a large degree do as they please. So, law or no law the real disciplinarian that truly protects and safeguards the culture, morals, and spirituals values in free nations are the economy.

We in the USA have a weak P . . . . of an economy that can't even protect itself from inflation let alone protect the nation's culture, morals or anything else. Right now, in the USA we have strong laws on the book to stop illegal immigration, crime, and every vice you can think of, yet, damn near everything is out of control. This could never happen with an economy with any teeth or bite.

All you have to do is look back before our liberal induced welfare state and nothing was out of control, which ought to tell you something. The most important thing in maintaining a civil and orderly society is the proper raising of the young, with a balance of love and discipline. In a free nation the economy must be free and untied to maintain discipline.

Cold Steel Raw Truth About White Liberals & Race In USA

Economic discipline is what safeguards and protects a nation's culture, morals, and everything else. With a true free market place economy things like the boom and bust cycle and even depressions occasionally are normal. To keep life fit to live nature must have ways to get rid of waste, moral decay, and inefficiency.

Otherwise, there can be no rebirth or re-growth. Then it may be all the way back to the Stone Age the way we are headed. It is even possible for man to disappear from the globe. I could go on and on, on how important a true free market place economy is to the survival of any free nation, but I will start closing this down.

We must untie and free our economy from what the shallow minded liberals did to it by enacting this evil 1938 socialist minimum wage law. What that evil law did was take the strength and power to fight off inflation away from the USA economy. And even today the USA economy doesn't have the power or strength to fight off inflation, let

Cold Steel Raw Truth About White Liberals & Race In USA

alone protect the nation's culture and morals.

The economy the USA has today is an almost useless, weak, p . . . . of an economy, not a strong kick-ass disciplinarian job producing machine that produced the roaring twenties. Only repealing the evil 1938 socialist minimum wage law can save this great nation. I can only pray that wise men/women will do their duty to save our beloved country.

My extremely wise supernatural wisdom is as threatening to the republican establishment as it is to the liberals and Dem's in my view. You can love me or hate me, but my only concern is the survival of my country. And I'm one that still truly believes in duty, honor, country above all else.
SIRMANS LOG: 02 OCTOBER 2014, 1543 HOURS

GREAT WRITER FREDDIE L SIRMANS SR GIVES THE ROCK-HARD COLD-STEEL TRUTH ON DOMESTIC ABUSE

Cold Steel Raw Truth About White Liberals & Race In USA

All I hear is abuse, abuse, wife abuse, child abuse, women abuse and on and on to no end. Liberal women are almost up in arms; and if it were left up to them they would de-nut all men and make sissies out of all of us. To me there is no mystery here, men are just being men, and it is just cause and effect in action in my view. Men are aggressive creatures by nature and are only doing what they are allowed to get away with. And it is a pipe dream to expect law enforcement to do more than put a dent in it.

It takes fighting fire with fire to really stamp out or completely get under control domestic type violence of this sort. It takes a lot of loved ones that are willing to make a personal sacrifice to truly stamp out or control domestic violence. There has always been some domestic abuse but never out of control like what we are seeing today.

What we are seeing today is the result of a lack of the strong nuclear and extended family unit. Today we have too few no-none-sense kick-ass dads or brothers that are prepared to go to hell or prison before they will tolerate this sort of abuse on a love one. We are too busy using the "N" word on each other to give a damn. Very few cousins or good friends are prepared to make such a sacrifice.

I have personally heard a few men say that the only thing keeping me off her ass is her dad would kill me. Sure, law enforcement will do their job and enforce the law, but no law enforcement agency can protect private citizens 24-7 day in and day out. Even if women are the weaker sex old man colt solved that imbalance many, many years ago by creating an equalizer. But, the thing about that is not all of us have the will or the guts to send a S.O.B. to hell.

SIRMANS LOG: 19 SEPTEMBER 2014, 2216 HOURS

It really is a waste of time trying to get a liberal to understand freedom and a free market place. That is why most of the world is poor and will always be poor. The point I'm making is liberals don't really understand freedom. Freedom means every individual has a

Cold Steel Raw Truth About White Liberals & Race In USA

free choice. Jobs don't just drop out of heaven, someone just like you and I must create or provide a job.

This is the land of the free and no one puts a gun to anyone's head and forces them to work for minimum wages. Everyone in this great country has the right to create his/her own job or quit any job one doesn't like. Most liberals think it is wrong for some people to enjoy the rich life while most stay poor. Right now if the liberals had the power they would take almost everything from the rich and spend it on social programs.

They are too shallow minded to realize that rich people are not stupid. They really believe rich people would continue producing and providing jobs while almost all of their earnings are being taken away. I just can't understand how anyone with any common sense could be so shallow, but they are, and are running the country, too.

There never has and never will be a rich and wealthy nation without a lot of

Cold Steel Raw Truth About White Liberals & Race In USA

rich greedy people to make it happen. If left entirely up to the liberals the USA would in no time be a third world nation. Yet, enough wanting something for nothing voters keep the tax and spend liberals in power while the country goes to hell in a hand basket.

SIRMANS LOG: 12 JANUARY 2014, 2341 HOURS

A HALF OF A LOAF IS BETTER THAN NOTHING! IF YOU THINK IT'S GETTING BAD NOW WITH OBAMACARE, YOU HAVEN'T SEEN NOTHING YET, YOU JUST WAIT, IF THE DEM'S WIN ANYTHING IN NOV. 2014, THEN WE WILL GET THE FULL THROBBING PURPLE SHAFT FROM THE DEMOCRATS. THEY WANT TO FIRST SECURE THE 2014 MIDTERM ELECTION BEFORE THEY RAM THE FULL SHAFT TO US. IT WILL BE EVEN LESS JOBS AND A TRILLION MORE IN DEBT. IT WILL BE LIKE DETROIT CITY NATIONWIDE! THINK ABOUT IT, WE WILL THEN GET ALL OF OBAMACARE,

Cold Steel Raw Truth About White Liberals & Race In USA

AND DRY, TOO. GOD, I ASK IN YOUR NAME SAVE THIS GREAT NATION.

It doesn't bother me a lot when I don't sell a lot of books. That is because I estimate only around 2 percent of the American population has the depth and wisdom to truly understand what the hell I be talking about. So be it, I carry on.

They can't get pass the fact that it is not the amount of money that truly matters; it is the buying power that really counts. Before the New deal which started the welfare state $5.00 would buy more than $50.00 will today.

Repealing the minimum wage law would put the provider role back into the hands of the people and allow this great country to survive. Otherwise, there is no way in hell the USA is going to survive on its present course.

Cold Steel Raw Truth About White Liberals & Race In USA

Just keep on believing in this phony minimum wage economy and without a doubt within a year I will be proven right. We'll soon see just how nutty my predictions are.

The repeal of the minimum wage law is our savior, but 98 percent of the population can't get pass believing more and bigger is always better. But, to me a half of a loaf is better than nothing because nothing is what this nation is going to get if we don't change course.

SIRMANS LOG: 29 DECEMBER 2013, 1022 HOURS

MAN/WOMAN OVERBOARD, USA ECONOMY SHIP IS BEGINNING TO SINK!

Folks, I'm just a lowly unknown writer out here pounding away trying to get through to thick sculls. Very few actually know about me or my books, and most of those that do are not interesting in tough accountability and responsibility. But, I know without a doubt at some point my writing will be vindicated.

Reality is reality there is just no way of getting around that fact. Sure, sometimes it takes a while for the results to catch up but there are no free rides in life someone always pays. The liberals and Dem's have been very successful; they have created masses upon masses of government dependents. They have convinced these dependents that government will always be there to take care of them and their needs.

That is not reality that is the biggest lie that has ever been told. There has never been a government that didn't go broke at some point. The free market place made the USA the most richest and powerful nation to ever exist. The government didn't do that, the free market place did that? Now, I believe most of the people running our government today doesn't even believe in a free market place.

I believe most of the people in charge of our government today are socialist or communist at heart. Everyone seems to be so surprised about how the liberals and Dem's connived and forced Obamacare down our throats. There is nothing new here about liberals in my view. How in the hell do you think the liberals and Dem's held on to the USA house of Representative for 40 consecutive years.

They did it by lying and conniving, and that is what is really happening with this Obamacare website. They will never let it work right before the November 2014 election. They intend to keep the confusion going and never let all of the high costs be widely known before the 2014 election. But, God help us if the Dem's win anything in November 2014, because if they do they are going to ram the full purple shaft to this free nation, e.g. Obamacare dry like it or not.

I believe these people are hardcore ideologues and will go down with the ship before yielding an inch, and believe me that is exactly what is about to happen. Trust me, this USA economy ship is taking on too big of a load and is beginning to sink. This ship is going down unless most of its government load is jettisoned, and fast.

However, the only way to lighten government's load is to kick it out of its social and family provider role. And the way to do that is repeal the minimum wage law or else, this economy ship is going down. I suspect many of the rats have already left the ship in spirit and have property in in places like New Zealand and Australia.
SIRMANS LOG: 26 DECEMBER

Cold Steel Raw Truth About White Liberals & Race In USA

2013, 1840 HOURS

WHO IS THE AFRICAN AMERICAN COMMUNITY'S DADDY?

I'm fixing to briefly weigh in on something I have no business touching, besides, some people think of me as a nut case anyway. What if I am off the beaten path that doesn't mean my beliefs are wrong. Even a broken clock is right twice a day. Concerning two great black athletes that are at loggerheads: Long before O. J. got into trouble, guess who was always on his case for being too white? Go figure? Some people just naturally goes against the grain, enough said. The problem with the African American race as a whole is culture.

The welfare state has destroyed the African American family structure and community. But, that don't mean we have to take it lying down and still not

Cold Steel Raw Truth About White Liberals & Race In USA

feel responsible for our own behavior and survival. I don't have the power to stop anything, but you can bet your bottom dollar that I will never make excuses for bad behavior. And no matter who does it I'm not accepting any excuses because of what happened in the distance past.

Grow up African Americans and take responsibility for the behavior of yourself and that of your race. This welfare state has destroyed accountability and responsibility throughout all of America and I'm sick and tired of it. Today a decent law abiding black man can't walk into many stores without being feared because we as a race won't clean up our own community house.

Don't tell me that ain't from a lack of feeling responsible for our own behavior as individuals and as a race. We still have a dependent slave mentality and think it's the white mans fault. The only cure for that is for someone to kick the crutch from under us and demand we stand on our own two feet. Independent minded people don't look to blame and find excuses to fail. I know I may sounds cold, but this USA economy is fixing to collapse and we black folks need to wake up and be prepared, now.

Every preacher in the pulpit and any member in the black community with an ounce of authority need to feel responsible for this cancer in our community called crime. I don't mean taking any physical action we have law enforcement for that. What I'm talking about is taking a moral stand instead of not feeling racially responsible for bad behavior in our youth.

If we don't save our youths no other race will. I didn't intend to vent like this, I just got carried away but something's need to be said. The so-called African American leadership is

out to lunch.
SIRMANS LOG: 18 DECEMBER 2013, 1750 HOURS

THERE IS NO GOVERNMENT SYSTEM EVER TO EXIST MORE SELF-DESTRUCTIVE THAN A WELFARE STATE!
Like a junkie on the streets trying to get a fix there is nothing a welfare state won't sell off to support its seized social and family provider role. As long as the USA government stays in its social and family provider role it will be impossible for the USA to stop reckless spending or survive.

Right now, the liberals don't have the survival instinct or the wisdom to see a real need to stop spending. They are living in the moment and can't see any real danger in reckless spending, and you couple that with an economically ignorant mainstream press and general public, all I know to do is pray.

Cold Steel Raw Truth About White Liberals & Race In USA

Abolishing the minimum wage law will give the social and family provider role back to the people where it belongs and has always been until the "New deal" seized it in 1938. God I ask in your name, "Save the USA." Time is a winding down, I don't know how much we have left, but I know beyond a shadow of doubt that a total economic collapse is near unless drastic changes are made.

When I look at the future I think the republicans will soon get the power to have their shot at this health care thing. But, I have news for them too, just like the Dem's they think government can keep and hold on to its social and family provider role, wrong.

I believe unless the republicans and conservatives set about abolishing the minimum wage law they will be seen as phony liberals and quickly replaced.

Cold Steel Raw Truth About White Liberals & Race In USA

But, of course do like the Dem's never admit in advance what your real intentions are, just git in there and rid the country of this Minimum wage law. It's a free market place killer. See Sirmans survival plan further down.

Most of the big cities water, sewage, and bridges infrastructure were built before a minimum wage law, so, don't tell me junking the minimum wage law won't save this great nation. And here is the real kicker: The USA economy is still the economic engine of the world and if it collapses it takes the world economy down with it. Sure, the world economy may bail us, but not before owning us.

The apple cart has been upset and the only thing that can save the USA is a true free market place. Pure communism and socialism never has and never will work, but, now we have a new monster far worse than both of those systems to contend with, it's called the welfare state. There is no system ever to exist more self-destructive than a welfare state.

It leaves almost no survival tools in place to survival on when nature's bust cycle comes around or if the economy collapses. It really is no joke when I say it may be all the way back to the Stone age for modern civilization. We have no strong nuclear and extended family system to survive on. We have centralized factory farming for our meats and vegetables and hardly any small farmers and home gardeners.

That means we have no adequate emergency backup bartering capacity if the economy collapses and money is worthless. And on and on, our family morals and values would make dog eat dog look like a Sunday picnic after a week into a collapse. Wages and prices must be free floating for a genuine free market place to work and that can't happen with a minimum wage law or any kind of wage or price control.

The consumer cost of living is what's going to kill off the USA economy and Obamacare just speeds up the process. Here is the Ultimatum: Either the USA government abolish the minimum wage law which will free the people to save themselves and the country, or it tries to consolidate and hold on to its current social and family provider role.

If it chooses the latter there is no doubt in my mind that it will to no avail sell off the country to foreigners to try to hang on to a role it shouldn't be in, in the first place. You just watch, and the wait won't be very long. I can dissect an economy as well as anyone and that is what I predict is going to happen. You can't get blood out of a turnip.

I doubt there is any gold left at Fort Knox and there is no telling what else has already been sold off by the

Federal Reserve. I'm telling you as a man of great super natural wisdom, unless the minimum wage law is abolished we might as well kiss our freedom and this great country good by forever.

SIRMANS LOG: 04 DECEMBER 2013, 2217 HOURS

AMERICA! YOU HAVE BEEN SOLD A FALSE BILL OF GOODS

There is a sucker born everyday. It amazes me how gullible people are. They have fallen for this cock & bull big lie that the Obamacare website is somehow a big screw-up, wrong. I for one don't buy that for one second. A computer or a website must obey what it is programmed to do.

The problem is: There is no way in the hell liberals and Dem's are going to let it be known on a large scale the double and triple cost the people will face until after November 2014. Get a grip

Cold Steel Raw Truth About White Liberals & Race In USA

America; you have been sold a false bill of goods. And be prepared for a never-ending list of excuses, but, you will never get a proper working website with cost no matter what you are told. I rest my case.

SIRMANS LOG: 30 NOVEMBER 2013, 2216 HOURS

One thing that gives me an advantage over most people is the ability to penetrate through fog and bore to the core of an issue. A lot of people think some kind of tax fix is the answer to the nation's problems. And there are others that think some kind of convention of the states is the answer.

But, I'm here to tell you nothing is going to save the USA and western civilization unless the core root problem is dealt with. And through all of the fog and side issues I see it all alone standing there the core and root problem itself. The core and root cause for the coming doom and destruction of the USA and western civilization is: "Government in the role of social and family provider."

Now government is personally responsible for millions upon millions of mouths to feed. And with its power to tax and spend nothing is going to stop it from caring for it's dependents in that role, period. Never in 6,000 years of written history on a mass scale has a government taken on such a permanent burden before the "New deal" came along.

Even in socialist and communist countries there are make work jobs. And until the USA government surrenders the provider role back to the private sector nuclear and extended family system this nation cannot and will not be saved from total doom. However, the big problem is acquiring the vehicle to get us back to depending on the bread and butter nuclear family system before our USA government crashes and burns.

The only vehicle on earth with the power to get the USA back on track is the all mighty all-powerful free market place. However, with the USA there is problem, the USA has a P . . . . of an economy.

No problem that can be fixed, the USA economy is just hog-tied and has no power to discipline itself due to the evil 1938 socialist minimum wage law. And that can easily be remedies by repealing the evil 1938 socialist minimum wage law, then a free untied all powerful free market place economy will take it from there and save this great nation.

Even on an individual basis a head of household provider is going to do everything within his/her power to feed and care for his/her dependents. There have been many cases where a family provider would beg, borrow, and steal to feed its dependents. So, it only stands to reason with government's power to tax and spend nothing is going to stop it from taxing production and producers to death to feed its dependents.

The only way to deal with government as a family provider is to get it out of that role, period.

Cold Steel Raw Truth About White Liberals & Race In USA

ADD ON: 17 SEPTEMBER 2014, 1004 HOURS

The private sector nuclear and extended family system is the only thing that can carry the social and family provider load over the long haul, period. Through shallow minded ignorance the liberals put this load and burden on a permanent basis on the USA government and it has been there ever since the "New deal."

Now, it has simply become too heavy for the USA government to carry it any longer, which is going to make it impossible for the USA economy to survive. There is simply no doubt in my mind the USA economy is going to soon crash, and our only hope is to repeal the evil 1938 socialist minimum wage law before it is too late.

If that is done in time that will transfer the load and burden back where it has always been for over 6,000 years with the private sector. And that will free up government to collect taxes, protect the interior, fight wars, etc.. That is the only thing that is going to save our

Cold Steel Raw Truth About White Liberals & Race In USA

USA P . . . . of an economy from a total collapse and soon.
We have no other choice if the great USA is to survive, period.
SIRMANS LOG: 16 SEPTEMBER 2016, 1348 HOURS

RAY RICE EPISODE, SEPT. 14, 2014 ADD ON, SCROLL DOWN
As a rule I stay away from commenting on hot button emotional issues, but to me it seems to be something sinister going on with this Ray Rice case and I decided to weigh in. Like it says in the good book let who is without sin throw the first stone seems to be totally forgotten.

No decent self-respecting human being is going to condone a vastly more powerful man knocking a woman out for any reason, period. However, we all are human and to err in itself is human.

If provoked enough we all have a snapping point, then you couple that with possibly two intoxicated individuals, who is to say who is victimized, here, reality is reality. Sure, punishment is due, but to take a man's lively hood away and totally destroy him for bad judgment and possibly too much to drink is overkill in my view.

People tend to live on a standard equal to their income and he probably owes a lot of people a lot of money. It is hard enough now for a woman to get a man to make a commitment, and crucifying punishment like this means passive type women are in and aggressive independent type women are out, reality is reality.

What concerns me about the whole thing is this liberal created political correctness hogwash. If this political correctness nonsense continues we will end up with a P . . . . of a nation just like we already have a P . . . . of an economy.

I will stop here; I have already said too much, I hope I don't end up begging on the streets due to the political correctness mob like what they may do to Ray Rice.

Cold Steel Raw Truth About White Liberals & Race In USA

These shallow minded liberals don't understand profit, individual freedom, or anything, they think survival is a pie train, almost everything in this great nation is upside down, God help us.

ADD ON: SEPT. 14, 2014
All of this ado and emotional hype about this case is not from football fans and the general public in my view. I think it is extreme liberalism gone amok. I see this as an individual case that has been turned into a mountain out of a molehill. But, extreme liberalism want to turn it into some kind of domestic violence movement.

Culture-wise we are past the point of no return when one can't spank or discipline one's child anymore, that in itself is a threat to law enforcement everywhere, but liberals are too shallow to see that.

When undisciplined youngster that have never been conditioned to act with restraint when dealing with frustration reach adulthood only law enforcement stands between them and an orderly safe environment.

Cold Steel Raw Truth About White Liberals & Race In USA

A child's basic personality is shaped by the age of six and many a first grade school teachers can point out even at that age the ones that will most likely end up in prison. That is our welfare state and liberalism in action.

Spare the rod you spoil the child is as valid today as it was 2000 years ago. Liberalism has destroyed this great nation and I'm just one lone neurotic mentally handicapped cripple trying to make a stand.

I don't expect most people to agree with me, but think God we live in a country where I won't disappear in the middle of the night. Praise be to God.
SIRMANS LOG: 12 SEPTEMBER 2014, 1559 HOURS

CONSERVATISM VERSUS COLD REALITY
I consider myself to be conservative, but even more so a realist. In terms of gaining and keeping power I think the establishment republican party is taking the right course.

Cold Steel Raw Truth About White Liberals & Race In USA

However, I also think the conservatives and tea party is right on what is best for the long term survival of our nation, but their policies will guarantee that the Dems stay in power and they never get power. The Dems created our welfare state and with them in power the good old USA will never get control of suicide spending.

With the establishment republicans in power the suicide spending train to hell will be slowed down considerably but not enough to avoid eventually reaching doom. My heart and soul is with the conservatives and tea party because they know this country's survival is at stake, but they are eighty years too late to make a do or die stand.

Conservatives allowed the liberals to enact two "New deal" programs that this great nation will never recovery from unless they are eliminated and soon. The first program was government seizing and taking on the role of social and family provider. That means government starts feeding on itself and taxing production until there is nothing left to tax. Duh?

The second program was enacting the cruel evil 1938 socialist minimum wage law. The cruel and evilness of this law means the death of a true free market economy, that is why I drumbeat so hard on ridding this nation of this monster.

This law alone is what allowed the shallow brained liberals to cripple the USA economy to the point it don't have the power to fight off inflation, which lead to the destruction of our culture, morals, and values. A true free market economy without a choking minimum wage law would never allow hoards of foreign invaders to flood into this great country.

That is because the demand wouldn't be there. Those now on welfare would have all of those jobs the invaders are seeking. And there wouldn't be any welfare for anyone to free load on; an unshackled free USA economy would never tolerate it. Sure, we have a welfare state today but I guarantee

Cold Steel Raw Truth About White Liberals & Race In USA

you we won't have one very much longer. Yet, we march on deeper into fantasyland.

Otherwise, the strong nuclear and extended family system, churches, and social organizations would be strong enough to meet social needs like through out history. And temporary government help would only be a last resort. Now, when this welfare state soon totally collapses the USA and western civilization may fall all the way back to the Stone Age. Wake up America, I'm for real, this is no joking matter.

The liberals from both political parties created this entitlement gimmy, gimmy populace as huge as ninety percent to some degree. So, lets face it, most of these masses of government dependents will never bite the hand that feeds them.

Sure, in some cases hardcore conservatives and tea party members are going to get elected, but to become a majority party in power ain't going to happen. I will sum it up by saying anyone that has read my work knows I offer a solution. And I know it will take a miracle for my solution to happen.

I don't know how the almighty is going to make it happen but I believe some way some how it will happen, it must. The evil 1938 socialist minimum wage law must be repealed it is the only solution.

Repealing the minimum wage law will set free the might USA economy that is still shackled and tired up from the evil 1938 socialist minimum wage law. No other force on this earth has the power to save the USA from total doom.

A free genuine true free market place economy has never failed to save a dying nation. Don't doubt me; my destiny is to keep sounding the distress call for survival.

Unlike authoritarian type governments, free countries with private property rights must rely on the free market place to maintain discipline and protect its culture, morals, and values. That is because people have the right to be stupid or anyway they want to be.

Right now 95 percent of the American people believe a higher minimum wage and making more money will solve their problems. That is like treating ones big toe thinking it will solve a heart problem.

The fact is its not how much money one makes that matters, it is far more important how much can be bought with the money one does make. The path we are on is fast destroying what little buying power our money has left. It actually happened in Germany where it took a wheelbarrow load of money to buy a loaf of bread.

There is no mystery on what ails the USA economy, the answer is very simple, the USA economy is totally out of balance, period. All that is necessary to set the USA economy back in balance is to set it free.

We set it free minus the choking and crippling 1938 minimum wage law, and then the economy will balance and fix itself. That is if government just stays the hell out of the free market place, and stay with collecting taxes.

Don't doubt me, there is no other way to save the USA no matter what the learned economist and egg heads tell you. Nothing in nature can exist without completing some form of rebirth cycle, and the USA is long over due.

SIRMANS LOG: 28 AUGUST 2014, 2246 HOURS

WHY MOST AFRICAN AMERICANS WILL NEVER VOTE REPUBLICAN?
African Americans are bonded to the Democrat party like a mother and child. And any Republican that thank he can break that bond is fooling himself. It is an exercise in futility; it can't be done by an outsider.

I'm no scholar on the subject, but I am a great thinker with super natural wisdom. I see mother and child like bonding as a phenomenon in nature. Super strong bonding doesn't just happen by accident there is a care taking survival element involved.

Sure, when born a mother may love her baby because it is hers but the super strong bonding builds from day to day caring for it. In fact a stray animal, plant, or anything that one feeds and provide water will bring about a bond and deep caring for it.

Two equals tend not to bond. Two dependents tend not to bond. The strongest bonding tends to occur when there is a provider and a dependent. An unselfish provider will always try to wean a dependent to become independent and stand on his own.

The mother eagle provider break the bond by kicking her young out of the nest thereby forcing them to provide for themselves. African Americans are mentally in the nest of the democrat party and that is where we will stay as along as the welfare state keeps the masses of social programs going.

As to the republicans, never mind the nation being bankrupted, you are the enemy for being too stingy. However, there is a real problem for the Dems, this thing called "Reality" keep trying to raise its ugly head. The reality is the USA is dead broke and can't continue footing the bill for mass provider and social spending.

The liberals are already gutting the military like Western Europe has already done to free up funds. I keep providing the solution but no one wants to hear it because it doesn't fit our mass economic ignorant thinking.

I will repeat it for the umpteenth time, repeal the evil 1938 socialist minimum wage law, now, that will set the USA economy free and it will save us all. Through out history a true genuine free market place has never failed to save a nation by producing jobs and more than enough of everything a nation needs.

Otherwise, we go down, we are all doomed when this great nation's economy soon collapses. Don't doubt me; I can dissect an economy as well as anyone.

Cold Steel Raw Truth About White Liberals & Race In USA

SIRMANS LOG: 26 AUGUST 2014, 1639 HOURS

IT IS NO LONGER A MATTER OF THE USA ECONOMY COLLAPSING, IT IS NOW WHO IS GOING TO OWN US

I keep harping on this evil 1938 socialist minimum wage law that almost everyone thinks is a good thing. And again I will repeat I am one hundred percent dead sure that repealing this law is the only thing that can save the USA from total doom.

I am at my wits end, where is our survival instinct as a nation, It's sheer madness the true state of the USA economy, yet we march on like zombies. Never before in history has a civilization allowed it nuclear family structure, culture, and moral values to be almost totally destroyed like what has happen with western civilization.

Western civilization has allowed liberal thinking to flim flam its citizens into thinking the welfare state will always be there to take care of everyone from cradle to grave. Yet, liberals hate profit and have never understood profit, which is the engine of economic survival.

Anyone that doesn't understand the role profit plays in a healthy economy is living in fantasyland and can't be trusted in my view. So, when I tell you the evil 1938 socialist minimum wage law is evil you had better believe it.

This nation's sheer survival depends on if and how we get rid of the evil 1938 socialist minimum wage law, period. Power and economics on an individual basis or as nation goes hand in hand.

The true evil of the 1938 socialist minimum wage law is it took the real power away from the economy and the people and gave government almost absolute power. When government can demand what a business must pay it workers no matter how small the economy can no longer protect itself or the nation's inner fabric.

If not for the evil 1938 socialist minimum wage law liberal propaganda

Cold Steel Raw Truth About White Liberals & Race In USA

could never have wielded the power through big government to destroy our nuclear family system, our culture, and our moral and spiritual values.

With no minimum wage law the USA economy would have had the disciplining power to fight off inflation and big government reckless spending; now USA currency is inflated out of sight.

The evil 1938 socialist minimum wage law must go so the USA economy will again be "Free at last, free at last" to save our nation. Otherwise, it is no longer a matter of the USA economy collapsing, it is now a matter of who is going to own us.

Folks, I am just a lonely self-made writer, I writer what I think and believe. Sure, some of my views are far fetched; still even a broken clock is right twice a day, think about it.
SIRMANS LOG: 25 AUGUST 2014, 1824 HOURS

Cold Steel Raw Truth About White Liberals & Race In USA

FERGUSON MISSOURI SITUATION HAS NATIONAL IMPLICATIONS!

As a self-made writer I believe this little flare up in Missouri has national implications. I believe that is why they can't seem to get a lid on the situation.

With a live or die election right around the corner I think the whole thing has become totally political. The Dems back's is against the wall and they are taking no chances. They feel their bread and butter most loyal supporter turnout must not be jeopardized.

So, they are hoping the situation slowly burns itself out. The last thing the Dems need is to have a mad base this close to November. However, in my view I think the Dems biggest threat not only in this case but also in life itself is "Reality."

The reality in all of the USA today is, if we as a nation don't control crime and violence it is going to soon control all of us. Enough said, I rest my case, the jury is still out.

Cold Steel Raw Truth About White Liberals & Race In USA

SIRMANS LOG: 19 AUGUST 2014, 1301 HOURS

WILL SOME AFRICAN AMERICANS SIT OUT THE NEXT TWO NATIONAL ELECTIONS?

I think the next two national elections will determine the survival of the USA as a free nation. I also think the next two national elections are the republicans to lose.

The Dems are going to have a big, big problem distancing themselves from their leader, which I think they are beginning to do. Everyone knows that the African Americans vote almost always goes ninety percent plus to the Dems. And most African Americans will never vote republican under any circumstance, which I think is a pity.

To me that show a survival dependency mentality that was born in slavery. It blocks freethinking and keeps one from feeling responsible for ones own survival. It leaves us blacks mentally dependent on the good white man (Dems) instead of ourselves for

Cold Steel Raw Truth About White Liberals & Race In USA

our survival.

Before the "New deal" blacks were more free thinking and independent minded, and even owned far more in wealth and property than today. But, somewhere after the "New deal" the republicans got branded the enemy and the Dems became our lord and savior. Me, I feel blessed and thankful in spite my troubled soul.

Being mentally dependent minded is why we as a race irresponsible mass kill off each other. We call each other the distasteful "N" word and won't readily support each other in business when there is a choice, in fact we don't really have a survival need to love and care about each other.

That is what this welfare state beast has done to us blacks, it has taken away a survival need for us to need, love, and respect each other. Accordingly to the law of "Natural selection," anything-in nature that doesn't have a survival need, it start ceasing to exist until it's gone.

Cold Steel Raw Truth About White Liberals & Race In USA

Sorry folks, I got carried away; sometimes I start analyzing and go on and on. Now, I was saying the African American voters are the Dems most loyal supporters by far. But, I think the Dems may be skating on thin ice if they think they can kick their leader to the curb and African Americans will still turn out in droves.

Sure, most will never vote republican under any condition, but that don't mean many won't be sitting out the next two elections if not careful, here. That is all, just decided to offer some food for though, and I will leave it at that.

SIRMANS LOG: 12 AUGUST 2014, 1505 HOURS

BEFORE THE "NEW DEAL" THERE WAS NEVER A THREAT TO USA CULTURE, MORALS, AND VALUES!
A lot of people think the USA has always struggled with socialist and others wanting to change or destroy our system of government, and they are right, but there is a big difference in what happening today.

Cold Steel Raw Truth About White Liberals & Race In USA

The big difference today is our culture, morals, and values are shot all to hell. With a jury in court or voters in an election no one can truly predict how stupid the outcome may turn out.

Before the "New deal" the country went through all kinds of problems and threats but there was never a deadly threat to our culture, morals, and values. Believe it or not, the old saying that no country can afford guns and butter is really true.

That is why Western Europe has already chosen butter, and the USA is now headed that way at warp speed by gutting our military. The destruction of the inner fabric of the USA started when the government seized the social and family provider role for itself during the "New deal."

That was the first dagger stab to our culture, morals, and values. No form of government can survive very long by taking from produces and giving to non-produces, in time the load just becomes too great.

Cold Steel Raw Truth About White Liberals & Race In USA

The second deadly and fatal dagger stab to our culture, morals, and values was the enacting of the evil 1938 socialist "Minimum wage" law.

That was the coup de grace because a true genuine free-floating free market place economy not only safeguards and protects itself; it protects a free nations culture, morals, and values, too.

By enacting an evil 1938 socialist minimum wage law that crippled and took away the economy's power to discipline itself or the nation. That left the USA with a P. . . . of an economy with no power to discipline itself or fight off inflation.

That allowed the government to inflate our currency and grow government like never before. Sure, all of this government financial power boomed the economy and made masses of people happy, but was it really worth the total destruction of the nations culture, morals, and values. I personally don't think so, but I'm just one lonely neurotic two finger pecking self-made writer.

I will sum this article up by saying the only thing on earth that has a fighting chance of saving the USA from total destruction is repealing the evil 1938 socialist minimum wage law. And even then it will only give us a fighting chance to overcome four generations of liberal claptrap.

Anyone that doesn't think that norms and traditions matter; need to take a look at religions that have mandatory chants or prayers. That is their secret to remaining unchanged over thousands of years. And they won't ever change or deteriorate as long they keep the same norms and traditions going. Yet, we wonder what happen to the good old USA? Duh!

Wise men/women has always known that how you raise your young is not everything; it is the only thing in terms of long time survival, period.
Get a grip America. How can you expect the young to show self-restraint and act responsible when they have

Cold Steel Raw Truth About White Liberals & Race In USA

never been conditioned to show restraint and act responsible? Duh.
SIRMANS LOG: 06 AUGUST 2014, 1728 HOURS

THE ECONOMY: FIGURES DON'T LIE, BUT LIARS SHOW CAN FIGURE!
Folks, as an extreme and neurotic self-made writer I don't expect most people to understand my views. To the shallow I may seem negative or maybe even a cold hearted uncaring hater, but nothing could be farther from the truth.

In fact I believe I am sort of a savior in terms of helping this great nation survive the coming troubled times. My view on all of this great news involving the USA economy: Hog wash, hog wash, and more hogwash.

I heard a guy on the radio say that the USA government is a parasite and when a parasite grows larger than it's host it kills its host. I totally agree with the above statement, the USA government haven't got there yet, but

Cold Steel Raw Truth About White Liberals & Race In USA

is awful close. Our welfare state beast is fast destroying our job producing free enterprise economic engine.

Every day the USA government grows larger as our profit driven job producing business host sector dwindles smaller. Never mind what the learned economist and egg heads tell you, I'm telling you it is impossible for the USA economy to overall improve or be saved unless the evil 1938 socialist minimum wage law is repealed entirely.

Man alone can't save a dying economy, the same as a doctor alone can't save a dying patient, but a true free floating free market place economy can and will save itself along with it's host nation if unshackled and set free.

Our evil socialist 1938 minimum wage law ties up and restricts our free market place economy to the point where it can't discipline and save itself. And I'm here to tell you I don't care how much tweaking and fine-tuning they do nothing can save the USA economy unless it is set free of the evil

Cold Steel Raw Truth About White Liberals & Race In USA

socialist 1938 socialist minimum wage law entirely.

Good economy news: pure poppy cock, liberals always make things better before an important election, I suspect the cost of fuel will soon be coming down considerably. We all are doomed unless? You know what? We are losing our great USA and it impossible to be saved unless we do what must be done; there is no other way, period.
SIRMANS LOG: 31 JULY 2014, 1821 HOURS

WRITERS VIEW ON THE LAW.
The legislative branch makes the law. The judicial branch interprets
and enforces the law according to the constitution. The executive branch carries out the law as is as signed under oath, period.

Now, what the hell should it matter what's one political view is when it come to the laws. The law means exactly what it says in plain English not some subjective liberal hogwash.

What goes around comes around, and what's up today may be down tomorrow. Freedom can't survive with no respect for the law, period.

SIRMANS LOG: 23 JULY 2014, 0255 HOURS

CONSERVATIVES AND REPUBLICANS FACE A TERRIBLE DILEMMA!

The shallow minded liberals over the years has lied and connived to set the USA on a course to sure doom. In their minds the end justifies the means. And they are too shallow and lack the survival instinct to even know the damage they have done.

Most liberals see no threat or danger in spending and want to increase spending and borrowing to grow government even larger. It is beyond me how anyone can believe you can

Cold Steel Raw Truth About White Liberals & Race In USA

borrow and spend to no end, but liberals do, I shake my damn head.

They don't see a spending problem with this country at all and if allowed to will spend this great country out of existence, and blame it all on the republicans. My God! What a situation. So you can see, expecting liberals to be responsible and safeguard this nation is a lost cause.

On the other hand, conservatives have an even bigger problem. Conservatives can't seriously plead the case of, "Ignorance is bliss." Conservatives has the capacity and depth to see our great country is on a sure path to disaster.

Conservatives know we are spending ourselves out of existence but face a terrible dilemma on how to stop it. In my view far too many conservatives still want to do the normal right thing of cutting spending and reducing the size of government, wrong. If conservatives do that, they will politically cut their own throats.

Right now that is the worst thing conservatives can do, simply because the liberals has made almost the whole country government dependent to some degree. So, the smartest thing conservatives can do is hold their fire and bide their time before cutting anything.

Talking about controlling spending may work, but to talk about cutting spending and government in this dependent minded climate will definitely keep conservatives out of power.

This writer's position even if no one else agrees with me is conservatives should make it their goal to repeal the evil 1938 socialist minimum wage law. But, never attempt that unless there is a very good chance of success.

Cold Steel Raw Truth About White Liberals & Race In USA

Getting rid of the evil 1938 socialist minimum wage law is the only chance of saving the USA from total liberal doom. It shouldn't be planed or talked about just get the power, get in there and do it.

However, there is a big problem, the conservatives disagrees with my views just as much as the liberals.

SIRMANS LOG: 17 JULY 2014, 1605 HOURS

WRITER FREDDIE L SIRMANS SR. DIDN'T WANT TO, BUT JUST HAD TO VENT.
The system can only take so much before it breaks and if that happens we all are in trouble, rich, poor and everyone. I think right now if there is mass disorder our welfare state beast is going for an all out power grab.

The citizen's still has the vote at the present, but if chaos takes place we may loose that to never regain it. So,

Cold Steel Raw Truth About White Liberals & Race In USA

when I fill my destiny and keep sending out the stress call to repeal the evil 1938 socialist minimum wage law entirely somebody better listen.

The only thing that can save the USA and individual freedom is a genuine pure free-floating free market place economy, period. And the 1938 socialist minimum wage law is the only thing that is blocking that from happening.

The minimum wage law must be repealed or found unconstitutional or we won't survive the coming doom. I promise you I have the supernatural wisdom and survival instinct to know what I'm talking about.

Nothing and I mean nothing is going to save the USA from a total collapse and doom unless the minimum wage law is gotten rid of one way or another. If you don't believe me just keep on living, we'll all soon find out. We all see our system being put to the test; it can only take so much before something snap.

Cold Steel Raw Truth About White Liberals & Race In USA

The thing about a true free float free market place is it doesn't choose sides and has never failed to produce an over abundance of whatever is needed. Who you know or who is under the desk doesn't count if you don't produce.

I don't care if you are liberal, conservative, democrat, republican, or whatever, if we don't get this evil 1938 socialist minimum wage law repealed or found unconstitutional we all are going to perish. You disagree, great; we'll soon see who is right.

I know the general public will never understand getting rid of the minimum wage law entirely and I understand that, who wouldn't won't to make and take home more money, I know I do. That is why the very wise founding father made the USA a republic (If we can keep it).

But, what's at stake here is the survival of our country and way of life, and I repeat, there is no way under the sun the USA and individual freedom will survive with the evil 1938 socialist minimum wage law still in place, period.

SIRMANS LOG: 16 JULY 2014, 1639 HOURS

GREAT WRITER BREAKS HIS PEN AND WEEPS!
Folks, I seem to be some kind of freak of nature or the victim of some kind of cruel joke. I am blessed with all of this supernatural wisdom, but no one listens.

I'm jumping up and down, turning flips, screaming and hollering that the evil 1938 socialist minimum wage law must be repealed entirely or found unconstitutional if the USA is to survive.

Its just that simple, our minimum wage law won't allow for a free floating all powerful free market place economy which would discipline itself and the country, too.

Now, our socialist just like in Western Europe is gutting our military to grow bigger government. The U.S. military is

Cold Steel Raw Truth About White Liberals & Race In USA

the last uncorrupted great institution left in America, and it can't be rebuilt overnight.

In my eyes the future seems so dim. There is no doubt in my great mind, only a true free floating free market place economy can provide the necessary discipline to save the USA. All that is necessary is to get rid of the choking evil 1938 socialist minimum wage law, otherwise there is no hope.

To be earnest, deep down in my soul I don't think the minimum wage law will ever be repealed. Too few have the wisdom or the survival instinct to see past their noses now days. I break my pen and weep.

Only the strong survives. The USA is weak in spirit and is the reason we are being invaded. God save the USA.

There is nothing hard or complicated about solving the illegal children invasion problem. The answer is something I have been drum beating on for several years. Maybe there is a divine element about this whole thing.

After all, more people visit a house of worship here in the USA than anywhere in the industrialized world, maybe we are worth saving. The answer to the problem is very simple; just repeal our evil 1938 socialist minimum wage law.

I know, I know, that don't make any sense, where is the connection. You can't see a connection that is because not everyone has supernatural wisdom and can dissect an economy like this writer can. I'm telling you this type of problem can be unsolvable and may bring the USA to its knee.

You may not agree with the method that I advised, but just remember you have been advised how to solve this problem.

SIRMANS LOG: 12 JULY 2014, 1008 HOURS

FOAMING MAD WRITER RANTS ON, OR, MAYBE HE IS RIGHT?
I, great writer Freddie L. Sirmans Sr. rant on, or, is my super natural

wisdom the gospel truth on what will save America. What most people fail to understand is that any way of life will be destroyed in 4-5 generations unless the proper norms and traditions are taught to the young.

During the New deal the government seized the social and family provider role for itself, and from that time since the poor has become totally corrupted. Never in history have the poor murdered unborn babies in the womb, that was always done by the rich and well to do.

The poor has always needed children for labor and to be taken care of in old age. The poor black man was kicked out of the home and that left no one to teach and enforce norms and traditions in the black family unit.

That is why we have all of the insane killing in the black community, that is why there is out of control violence and disorder in the African American community. And it ain't going to get any better until government is out of the social and family provider business, period. Sure, do gooders will talk, talk it to death, but will never accept a remedy with any teeth in it.

Since the New deal this whole country is not the same country as before. The mentality is not the same anymore. Gone are the old fashion norms and traditions of depending on ones self. The welfare state has long sent any independent frontier like spirit packing.

Hell, almost half of the country thinks the government owes them a living. It's insane, like the USA government can't ever go broke; where in the hell did stupid thinking like that come from. Not only can the USA and world economy go broke, the USA is already there. The USA is living on borrowed time.

The USA doesn't have a pot to piss in. The USA is almost $18,000,000,000,000,000,000 in debt and counting. Due to our welfare state taking away the need for a strong nuclear and extended family system we have nothing to survive on if we

Cold Steel Raw Truth About White Liberals & Race In USA

can't borrow anymore, its sheer madness.

There never has and never will be a society or nation that survived without a dependable nuclear family system in place, period. Ours are in ruins. Our moral and spiritual values also are in ruins. Today's norm is murdering unborn babies in the womb on demand. And damn the future, just marry the same sex and ignore the fact that there is no future without procreation, who you love is more important than future survival.

What the hell is my problem, I must be mad or some kind of nut talking all of this normal stuff that was the norm 100 years ago. Your kind is not welcome in the year of our lord two thousand fourteen; go back to the twentieth century.

If the economy crashed tomorrow we have practically no emergency backup bartering capacity to buy time on. Call me a nut, kook or whatever, but I know I am right on my grave concerns. I beg and I plead, repeal the evil 1938 socialist Minimum wage law now, it is the USA only hope of survival on what's headed our way.

Call me stupid or whatever you like but you ignore my concerns at your own risk. Sometimes, I wonder, Is Washington an imaginary metropolis with a lot of kids behind the wheel.

SIRMANS LOG: 10 JULY 2014, 1732 HOURS

IS THE END NEAR FOR A FREE USA
When the USA is
17,000,000,000,000,000,000 in debt and going a trillion or more deeper each year, you are not going to convince me we have a great future or even a future at all. The USA is almost totally at the mercy of its lenders.

If nothing else, at least repealing the evil 1938 socialist minimum wage law would give us a genuine true free market place economy and that would assure our survival under all conditions.

Wake up America and get a tight grip

Cold Steel Raw Truth About White Liberals & Race In USA

on reality because this nation is fixing to have a very, very rude awakening. Liberalism, liberalism, liberalism, I shake my head.

These illegal immigrant people think they are coming to the USA promise land, so, what went wrong, who are to blame. As a writer, I don't know, but, I suspect the hidden hand is the Dems and liberalism.

Love, caring, and having a sense of compassion is good things and is the spice of life. Life would hardly be worth living without these things. However, these predominate feminine emotions make some problems practically unsolvable.

Most of us know what it is like dealing with a wayward family member. Being an enabler almost never helps. When everything else fails most families just let nature take it course. The same applies to the USA as a nation.

If the minimum wage law was repealed a true free market place economy would kick in and solve the immigration problem, our jobless problem, our social problems, and on and on.

In the end this immigration thing will boil down to a test of the USA character and survivability, will we pass the test? Not unless the evil 1938 socialist minimum wage law is repealed entirely.

I hope I'm wrong. Almost no one agrees with me on this, still, I stand by my prediction. This whole thing is bigger than Immigration alone, it will determine if the USA survives with individual freedom still intact.

Two primary things have allowed the shallow minded liberals to strike at the heart of our system of government and unless that is corrected there is no way possible for the USA to survive as a free nation.

Number one, by enacting the evil 1938 socialist minimum wage law it gave the USA a p . . .. of an economy with no power to discipline itself. Number two, by government seizing the social and

Cold Steel Raw Truth About White Liberals & Race In USA

family provider role for itself and not enforcing any rules or conditions, that left no one enforcing discipline and passing on norms and traditions for future generations.

A society can't just start over from scratch with each generation and expect to survive very long. The USA is falling apart from lack of sound judgment and character with fewer and fewer people with any common sense.

For example, the law. You don't obey the law because you like it, you obey the law because it is the law. The law is the only thing that protects us all, and especially the poor and powerless. The news media ought to be up in arms with the way the law is flaunted in our faces in high places.

It is impossible for this great nation to remain a free people with no respect for the law like what is happening in the USA today. I rest my case, the jury is still out, we'll see.

No one is above the law doesn't seem to apply anymore in the USA. The bill of rights and individual freedom is something almost unheard of in history before the USA came along, and I use to wonder why.

Now, after seeing what liberalism has done to the USA I understand why freedom is so hard to acquire and hang on to? I just chalk it up as nature knows best. Everything about nature and survival is geared toward struggle.

It is so easy and tempting to just take the course of least resistance and jump on the liberal pie in the sky bandwagon. But, I have sense enough to know that no nation can survive without a strong nuclear and extended family system, strong moral and spiritual values, and adequate emergency bartering capacity.

For 6,000 years until the liberal's new deal, governments had the sense to leave the social and family provider role in the hands of the nuclear family unit. Instead during the new deal the USA government removed the need for a strong nuclear and extended family system by seizing that power for itself.

Now, when this whole global economy comes crashing down there is no foundation left to prevent the USA from regressing all the way back to the Stone Age. To me this is common sense thinking, what's wrong with me for wanting to help save my country and survive, shame on me.

Government forcing a evil 1938 socialist minimum wage or price control on a private profit driven business is unconstitutional, period. Of course every worker would be a fool if he/she didn't want to take home more money.

But, force destroys a genuine true free market place economy and results in what's happening in the USA today with no jobs and galloping out of control cost of living. And the really sad part is it's only the tip of the iceberg before total collapse and doom.
SIRMANS LOG: 03 JULY 2014, 1908 HOURS

Cold Steel Raw Truth About White Liberals & Race In USA

THE END

FREDDIE L SIRMANS SR.
WEBSITE: FLSirmans.com

www.ingramcontent.com/pod-product-compliance
Lightning Source LLC
Chambersburg PA
CBHW051722170526
45167CB00002B/760